Painting with Light

Poetry and Prose
A Collective

Valentina

Trust will unleash her.

Painting With Light is a journey through faraway places and wild spaces. This collection will immerse you in the natural world and take you to sacred oceans. Valentina writes expressively about love and lust, romance and matters of the heart, in the energy of the moment. Igniting all the senses, this body of work is an eclectic mix of poetry and prose.

The Natural World

Twilight sky and current lines
life flows effortlessly
as the ocean breathes.

As the night tangoes
with the daylight
the stars begin to dance.

Reflections at the River Mouth

Sounds of silence.
But an oystercatcher
Calling to its echo

Tidelines and periwinkle trails
contour drawings in the sand
a warm glow bathes the land
reflecting the neon-blue sky

A school of salmon circles by
flowing in the eddies.
Sweeping wingspans, a pair of white-bellied sea eagles
call to one another as they glide,
home.

Flow

Frogs yawping in the creek
rejoicing that Spring is on its way
the flow, peaceful, calming me back to even keel
smooth rocks beneath bare skin

soothing, like a mother's tight embrace
fresh-vibrant, emerald-green moss
grows life on burnt driftwood
new hollows for new creatures

the wattle is in bloom
a gum towers over me and the creek a twisted
tangle of limbs
stretching up to cirrus clouds.
I take a deep breath and exhale

the sweet scent of flowering trees
crackling seeds
wildflower bulbs pierce the earth and spring forth
in all their splendour

freesias and jasmine adorn the landscape
an exotic perfumery
the water eddies, spirals and bubbles
carving sensuous shapes in the lay of earthen
rocks
nurturing and grounding

layers of algae, form lines beneath the surface
a small patch of gravel creates an island
water is life itself.

Spring

Chains of jasmine adorn the shrubbery.
Mating calls a-plenty as dawn breaks,
Courting Fairy Wren's elegantly dance in sync.
Honeyeaters collect nectar and
A possum takes a nap on the day lounger.
Sweet are the first scents of spring –

The cymbidiums are flowering beautifully,
Heirlooms from my Nonna's legacy.
Apple and peach blossoms
Line old country roads
The last of the Magnolia blossoms
Blow away in the breeze.

Whale mothers and calves
Breach in succession
Frolicking in the choppy seas of the windy months
I spot a baby seal
Floating, baking in the pre-summer sun
Twisting and turning making its own fun.

**Blessed
are
those
that
feel
blessed.**

Feeling Melancholic

Eb and flow
highs and lows
seasonal ...
cyclical.
I'm yet to know
flying high and solo
southerly buster
I'm bottoming out and so low

but it will not last.

I'll be afloat again

see blue skies again

feel the rain on my soul

and dance free of pain again.

Move to the vibrations

And pulsing natural beats

A Silent Mind

To glide like twilight
slide as silken drops across
a shimmering tide

glow as a rising moon
to be still as midnight
to just be

flow with the ocean of life
dance to its sweet, melodic rhythms

enlivened by her every breath
enchanted by her abundant life,
her sensuous curves
and flowing fountains.

Be the spark

Ignite the fire within your heart
The cauldron in your belly
And set your compass
To your true north

From the dark depths
to the shimmering light
ascending to the shallows
once again.

Grace

A kaleidoscope of butterflies
a pair of bright yellow sunbirds
creating sculptural nests
outside my kitchen window

Honeyeaters suckling nectar from grevillea flowers
a great egret takes flight
and lands gracefully
on the ephemeral pond

a family of red-bellied black snakes
recharge in the sun
entwined as one
a heron on the back of a bull
symbiosis in full
view, a mutually beneficial relationship

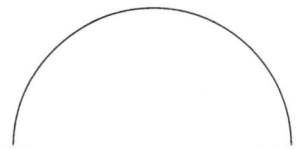

a symphony of birdsong at dawn
signalling I survived the night and I am safe.
a triggerfish protects its habitat
a curious dog on my morning beach walk

the dazzle of the sea
bright orbs of white light
a pod of dolphins emerges and swims by
the whales breach high
white ladies
upon the ocean swell

the first freesias
leap forth in all their beauty
the scent is intoxicating me
with the joy of the first days of spring.

Dancing Eyes Closed

Hip swivels and shimmies
sways and figure of eights
beckoning forth
the bounty of the universe

picking from the vines of delight
abundance
feeling and channelling in essence
summoning her.

LOVE
and Lust

Late Night Musings

Desire

Elusive or exclusive
Trust will unleash her
Free her
So I will be her

Honeyeater

Suckling on the sweetness of life
raw beauty
unravelling before my eyes
It's no surprise

I feel young again
I've found it
so let's again
begin this new adventure.

Nectar

Be my honey bee
my sweet nectar, my power
sting me with your seduction
like the sun to a flower

wet me with your rains of desire
bloom rose divine, I'm thine
hot rush, baby light my fire
pulsating rhythms of light

juicy, hot and sticky dark night
light me up brighter and brighter
electric dreams
The afterglow burns bright.

It's ignited something in me,

unleashed the angst.

Effervesce

Spilling over

stars sparkling on bare skin

nakedness from without

and nakedness from within

                                          a juiciness awakens
                                          surging desires am I forsaken
                                          release me
                                          please me

squeeze me
tightly, strong arms embrace
tear off my lace
skin on skin
moving deep within
me maybe for a second you are me
effervescence dazzles my flesh
should I repent
know now I'm content.

Was it lingering lust or love ...

Dazzle

Talk dirty to me.
Be gentle but love me hard.
Breathe me in
embrace

soak in a bath with me
swim naked, skinny surf
make love by the fire
take me in the kitchen

set fire to me on the dancefloor.
Allure, align
undress me with your piercing, blue eyes
seduce me with your longing stare
wind me up and then release me
keep going, it just gets better and better
higher and higher
then do it over and over
and again, take me there.

Bring

the

garden

back

to

life

after

she

lay

dormant.

Soulmate

You followed me
To Sydney
And I ran away

It was too uncanny
I freaked out
And now you're lost

Star, or Alter Ego

She's a beautiful soul
And not just pretty

Vibrant and zesty
Fabulously witty

Love her wildly,

Her darkness and her light.

Accept everything about her,
Including her shadow self

Even when she loses sight
Of the beauty of life

And the in-between of every moment
Between waking and sleeping,

Knowing and believing.
Love her to the depths of her soul.

Adventurer

You loved me
But I never really knew
So you made films of me

And I realised
But it was too late
It was already over.

I Was Young

I thought I loved you
But I had mistaken it for lust
A burning desire
To know you.

Elusive and wild

It was intense

and electric

Maybe I was just high

But now as time has swept by
I still feel that surge of desire
For what once was
In those younger days.

Blue Eyes

New Year's Eve
I was so naive
Some kind of love
Hit me like a brick
But it was lust
Or I was just high again.

Your sweet lips
I dream to smoulder over
Or watch you sleep,
Elation.
Then the hurt ran deep
So, to the depths
And back
You broke me
But I put myself
Back together,
a little more cautious
to love the same again.

Reconciliation

Love letters
Didn't heal
The piece of my severed heart

You took

But I found something else

I realised; I didn't need you anymore.

Mongolia

From the vastness of the steppes
to snow-capped mountain peaks

through the Gobi, to icy lakes
camels, yaks and desert snakes

Marrakech

Exotic and steamy
sweet and spicy
smoky and sultry
freezing and blizzardy

deserts, music and cobra snakes
in the medina dancers await.
mystics light frankincense
in the colourful souks,
from the quarter,
a hypnotic flute toots.

mosaic pots serve tagine on a plate,
the medina is awake tantalisingly late.
cooling on the kasbah rooftop
with tangerines and dates
film and rose festivals
I can't wait

Marrakech soulful
vibrant and gritty
East meets West
in the red city.

Cuba

Vibrant and lively
  zesty and resilient

    Warm and welcoming
     casa-mama's
     mighty mojitos and
     film festivals

    ballet, theatre and grimy bars
     reggaeton and revolution, the locals
   are all-stars

  cigar smoking gauchos out on the streets
  music and dancing spilling out to the beats

children dancing before they can walk
gigolos seducing and talking the talk

hitching in trucks or on the back of a bike
catch a ride in a Chevy and dance till light.

Swell

White horses charging forth
onto the shoreline
white ladies appearing before my eyes
with every gust of heavenly wind

Siren Song

She was deliciously zesty
and danced to the rhythm of life itself
sensuous and sultry
playful and ethereal

swimming in the sea foam
the souls of mermaids
she speaks to the sea
and dances with the waves

recharging at the waterfalls
and as she sings
the water reflects back to her
a beautiful, soul song
bareback on sea ponies
galloping along the seashore
raw natural beauty
eternally wild and free

She lives to be.

Wanderer

Collecting seashells
gifts from the sea
observing fractals
repetitive patterns in nature
sacred and calming on the mind
I begin to see
we are all intertwined.

Waterman

She loved the way he
danced across the wave
carving out wake lines
in a creative flow
on the sheer face of the wave
she felt his power

as he took his
deep bottom turns
and hit the lip
in aerial elegance
over and over again
shooting down the line

the lip foaming before him

he keeps the pace

in sync with the presence

of the swell line.

She, Part I

She too knew the feeling
of being immersed in
the raw energy
of the surf.
she rode a board too
but she preferred
to surf bare-skinned,
naturally for total freedom
in the waves of her

She, Part II

But her mind was like a wild brumby
charging down the snowy mountain pass
a fiery chestnut,
unsettled by the wind

although she relished
the luminescent waters
reflected by a stormy sky
mauve-grey cumulus nimbus floating by

rolling in, along the horizon
an electric,
hint of golden light in the clouds
carrying energy with the storm

she would charge up the beach
like a thoroughbred
darting in and out of the shore break
capturing the wildness, the energy
of the ocean
chasing the spirit of the sea
that fleeting feeling
of being
wild and free

Valentina:

*feminine noun from Latin origins,
name meaning 'strong.'*

Valentina is a spirited, intrepid traveller and storyteller. She is inspired by the wild places she has explored, particularly the oceans of her island home, Australia. She loves painting with words or penning a self-portrait in her own lyrical style, often deep in nature. Valentina's words are bold, reflective and offer a fresh take on poetry.

Visit Valentina on Instagram at @valentinapoetry4u.

Valentina

© Copyright 2024

Published by: La Societá
Edition: Printing of 1st edition, October 2024
Instagram: valentinapoetry4u
Design: ahoy-design.com

All rights reserved. No portion of this book may be reproduced in any form without written permission from the publisher or author.

ISBN 978-1-7635025-0-5

www.ingramcontent.com/pod-product-compliance
Lightning Source LLC
Chambersburg PA
CBRC091451160426
43209CB00022B/1870